Ormskirk
in old picture postcards

Mona Duggan

European Library ZALTBOMMEL/THE NETHERLANDS

GB ISBN 90 288 5399 5

© 1992 European Library – Zaltbommel/The Netherlands

Second edition, 2002: reprint of the original edition of 1992.

European Library

post office box 49

NL – 5300 AA Zaltbommel/The Netherlands

telephone: 0031 418 513144

fax: 0031 418 515515

e-mail:publisher@eurobib.nl

INTRODUCTION

This collection of postcards and photographs has been compiled to keep alive the memory of Ormskirk in the period from 1890 to 1930. Memories of what it was like to live in the town during those years are fading rapidly and very few people remain who have personal memories of 19th century Ormskirk. Such memories are part of our heritage and should be perpetuated.

Ormskirk has had many claims to fame — or notoriety — throughout the generations. In Tudor times, it was renowned as the centre of the glove trade and even in the 17th century, many townsfolk bequeathed gloves to their favoured relatives as a mark of special regard. After the Civil War and the disastrous siege of Lathom House, Ormskirk had a more macabre claim to fame. Visitors came from far and wide to see the tomb of James, the seventh Earl of Derby, who had been beheaded at Bolton in 1651. The vault of the Derby family in the parish church had two wooden doors which could be opened by visitors to reveal the two coffins; one containing the body of the unfortunate earl and the other the head. At the end of the nineteenth century the tomb was sealed and the church no longer provides this grim spectacle for visitors.

Other less gruesome happenings made the church memorable to certain groups of people in bygone years. For the Quakers, it was the scene of Oliver Atherton's courageous attempt to convert the townspeople in 1658. 'Moved by ye Lord' and without a thought for his own safety, he climbed into the pulpit immediately before the morning service and preached the faith of the Quakers to the gathered Anglican congregation. When the vicar approached, the constables jumped up from their pew, forcibly removed Atherton and escorted him to the Town Hall in Church Street, where he was imprisoned for a day.

For the Ormskirk Presbyterians, the eastern window of the church perpetuates the memory of their first great leader, Nathaniel Heywood, who was ejected from the church in 1662 for his puritanical beliefs. He was so highly respected in the town that on his death in 1677, the town constable led the vast crowd of people through the town to the parish church. The Anglican authorities allowed Reverend Starkie, a Presbyterian minister, to preach the sermon and Heywood was buried in the parish church in the burial place of the Stanley family, the Bickerstaffe chapel, now the site of the north aisle.

Others had less commendable reasons for remembering Ormskirk. The market place was the site of the pillary and stocks where many offenders were punished. Among those put in the stocks in the seventeenth century were the townsfolk who dared to talk during the meeting of the Court Leet, the forerunner of the Council. At the bottom of Aughton Street was a cook stool over what was then a much larger brook. Any woman who scolded or 'chid' in the township was punished by being ducked on the stool into Dyers' Lane Brook. There was a whipping post in Burscough Street and it was here in 1746, that John Halton was tied, stripped naked and whipped for drinking the health of the Pretender. Many other Jacobites remembered Ormskirk as the place where they raided a glass warehouse when they fled northwards during their retreat from Derby in 1745. They smashed dozens of glass bottles and scattered them on the roadway to impede the loyalist cavalry which was pursuing them.

Ormskirk and Lathom were also remembered for the curing properties of their waters. Towards the end of the 17th century and during the early years of the 18th century, Ormskirk was one of the early spa towns. Long before the emergence of such spas as Harrogate and Scarborough, the Earl of Derby saw the possibility of such developments and authorised the grounds around the spring at Lathom to be landscaped and music to be provided for dancing to entertain the visitors. Both the spring at Lathom and the cold plunge bath at the bottom of Greetby Hill were visited by those suffering from a wide variety of illnesses, seeking cures. William Blundell, the Cavalier, visited the spa, but found the cure very costly, for he felt so well that he ate all before him! The spring which fed the plunge bath was used, until recently, by the Bath Springs Brewery, where 'cures' of a different kind were prepared.

Other sources of entertainment were available to visitors to the town. Race meetings were held on Aughton Moss, where many of the gentry took their horses to challenge those of their neighbours. Gradually, these meetings grew into major events, attracting many spectators. Later, visitors were given the opportunity to take part in the fun, and races for footmen and even for the women, were introduced into the programme. Near the Beaconsfield memorial was a cockpit, which gave its name to Cockpit Lane between St. Helens Road and Chapel Street. Here, on many occasions, the celebrated Derby cocks challenged those of other Lancashire gentry. On other occasions, humbler cocks fought for the amusement and wagers of the crowd. Cock fights were often organised to coincide with the fair which was held twice yearly, at Whitsuntide and during the first week in September. Until the early years of this century, Ormskirk was famed for its horse fair, when people converged from all over Lancashire to buy or exchange their animals. Of course, all kinds of other things were sold: fairings – pottery souvenirs –, linen, cakes and sweetmeats. 'Quack' doctors often visited the fair hawking their remedies and conjurors demonstrated their tricks to the crowd. In earlier fairs, various exotic animals were displayed to the wonderment of the children and companies of players presented dramatic productions to the spectators. The whole memorable scene would be similar to that repeated nowadays in the large square at Marrakesh in Morocco.

Market day has always been an opportunity for enjoyment. People from the neighbouring villages gather to sell their wares and exchange news and townspeople take the opportunity to buy fresh produce from the countryside. Also on sale is the famous Ormskirk gingerbread which earned the town the title of 'Gingerbreadopolis'.

Most of these memories have faded as time has passed by, but, fortunately, we now have photographs to perpetuate the more recent memories for future generations. In the following pages we present a collection of postcards generously lent to us by Don Ambrose of Ormskirk, together with photographs and reminiscences of several kind friends and hope that these pictures will reawaken memories of the more recent past.

LATHOM HOUSE

1. Lathom House, a few miles outside the township of Ormskirk, has been closely associated with the town because it was the home of the Earls of Derby, the lords of the manor of Ormskirk. This building replaced the ancient Lathom House which was destroyed when the besieged Cavaliers surrendered to the Round-heads in 1645. Then in 1724 this house, designed by a famous Italian architect, Giacomo Leoni, was sold to Sir Thomas Bootle, a wealthy lawyer and Member of Parliament for Liverpool. During the First World War a re-mount depot was set up in the park to accommodate 7,000 horses and about 2,000 men. The build-ings suffered greatly during the army's occupation and since then they have gradually deteriorated until now only the western stable block remains. Plans are afoot to renovate these buildings, but a lot of con-troversy surrounds the project.

ORMSKIRK CHURCH

2. Ormskirk church is one of only three English churches with both a tower and a steeple. Many legends remain about its origins. The most popular is that two sisters could not agree on whether their legacy should be spent on a tower or a steeple. Eventually, a compromise was reached and both tower and steeple were erected. The more plausible explanation is that the spire was not strong enough to house the bells from Burscough Priory, given to the church at the dissolution of the monasteries. Consequently, the tower was built for them, using stones from the ruined priory. Beneath the east window can be seen an ancient stone built into the wall. Whether it was part of a Norse cross or Celtic-Romano carving is uncertain, but it is reputed to depict St. Paul in chains accompanied by a Roman soldier.

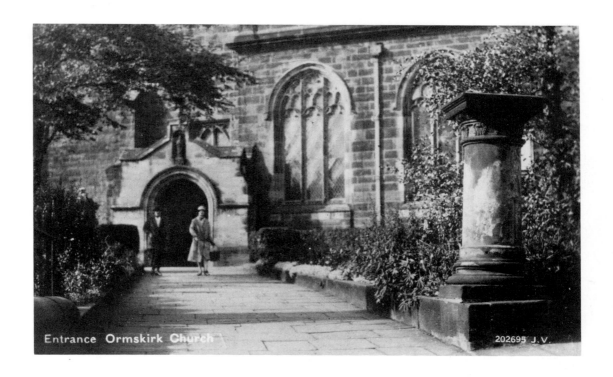

Entrance Ormskirk Church

202695 J.V.

3. The entrance porch to the church was built in 1891, after the children of the parish had collected £130 to pay for it. The daughter of the vicar's warden, Jane Maria Freeman, who was then only seven years old, laid the foundation stone and was presented with a silver trowel to commemorate the event. The pillar in the foreground was formerly one of the supports for the galleries inside the church which were removed during the renovations of 1885. At that time much of the ancient fabric of the church was removed to create a large, airy church.

4. This picture of the interior of the church shows two small galleries with rows of candles on them, either side of the east window. These have since been removed, leaving a plain wall which allows more light into the chancel. Here the lectern is in the form of a brass eagle, an allegorical reference to the word of God being carried down from heaven and also, incidentally, an echo of the eagle in the Derby coat of arms. In 1949 a carved wooden stand, a fine example of modern craftsmanship, took its place. The small lights above the choir stalls have also gone to make way for the modern lighting system which now graces the church.

CROSS HALL LATHOM

5. Although Cross Hall was in Lathom, it had so many connections with the history of Ormskirk that it warrants inclusion in this collection. This was the home of one branch of the Stanley family, who for many years held the right to the tolls from Ormskirk market. It was demolished in the early part of the 20th century and all that now remains is a section of the garden wall and the old barn which stood behind the house. This Hall stood on the corner of Ladies Walk and the road leading from Ormskirk to Westhead and has given its name to the hill on which it stood − 'Cross Hall Brow' − and later to the school built there − 'Cross Hall High School' − on the site of the old industrial school.

INDUSTRIAL SCHOOL ORMSKIRK

6. The industrial school for pauper children was opened on Cross Hall Brow in 1886. During the early years, the staff rose at 5.30 a.m., breakfast was served at 7.15 a.m. and then the dormitories were scrubbed each day by the children. The guardians provided clothes for the children, but the dress of the girls caused some controversy. The lady guardians thought that the girls were indecent without drawers and that some should be provided. The male guardians disagreed, declaring that women had not worn drawers for centuries and as many women, who continued not to wear them, were accepted as being perfectly decent, they felt the extra expense was quite unnecessary. After a heated argument, the lady guardians won the day and drawers were provided. In 1895, a more lenient board of guardians decided that scrubbing the floors each day was unnecessary and that breakfast could be served at 8 a.m.

ORMSKIRK 1918

7. As soon as the war broke out in 1914, the guardians announced that 50 beds could be provided at the industrial school for wounded soldiers and sailors at short notice. The offer was not taken up until 1917, when the children were moved and the hospital was opened. About 200 soldiers were transferred to convalesce at Ormskirk and in 1918 an annex, containing another 54 beds, was opened. The government only provided essentials for the soldiers and so the people of Ormskirk organised events to raise money for various comforts. Several townspeople entertained soldiers in their homes and, on at least one occasion in 1917, the soldiers were invited to the Golf Club where they played golf, bowls and various indoor games. The hospital finally closed on 30th April 1919.

Cottage Hospital, Ormskirk. 486

8. Before the workhouse on Wigan Road was converted into a hospital, the townsfolk were served by this cottage hospital in Hants Lane. Schoolchildren were treated for minor ailments in the clinic, which is towards the back of this picture. Later, this hospital was renamed the Brandreth Hospital, in memory of the famous Ormskirk doctor who was one of the leading physicians in Liverpool at the beginning of the nineteenth century. Dr. Brandreth also raised money to erect a new building in Burscough Street for the dispensary, which at the time was in Lydiate Lane (now Derby Street East). That extravagant piece of palladian-style architecture has since become the Farmers' Club.

BURSCOUGH STREET ORMSKIRK

9. This picture was taken from the roadway in front of the Buck i'th' Vine looking northwards towards Derby Street. On the right hand side was Wragg's the photographer's shop. He specialised in portraits of the town's worthies and sold cartes de visite which are now very collectable. Lower down the street, the notice 'CTC' can be seen outside Rudd's cycle shop where touring cyclists could obtain bed and breakfast accommodation. Derby Street crossed near the place where the horse and cart were standing and the shop with the canopy on the corner was Johnson's the greengrocer's. The tall house beyond the shop was Knowles House where Dr. Craig practised between the wars. The Council offices to the south of Derby Street can be seen towering above the man pushing a handcart.

10. Since this picture was taken, two properties — Johnson's, the greengrocer's shop on the corner of Derby Street and Burscough Street and Knowles House next door to it — have been demolished to make way for the county library. The small building on the right was the fire station. When the fire bell was rung, the volunteer firemen of the town — and anyone else available to help — would run to the station, fetch the horses from their stables in Railway Road, harness them to the pumps and rush off to the fire. Local boys were always ready to help man the pumps because they were paid a few coppers for their trouble. Earlier, the fire engine had been housed in a lean-to shed next to the house of industry on the corner of Moor Street and Chapel Street, on the site of Webster's furniture shop.

3372. DERBY STREET, ORMSKIRK.

11. At the other end of Derby Street was the Girls' National School, now converted into Stokers' furniture store. This example of Victorian gothic architecture was built by voluntary contributions and is a lasting memorial to the generosity and civic pride of our forefathers. It was 'capable of providing accommodation for 1,000 scholars', but the intention of cramming so many children into a building of that size shows how different ideas on education were in that era. Until the 1950s, when the new school was opened on Greetby Hill, this school served as a mixed infants and junior girls' school. The magistrates court building on Derby Street has altered little and the standard measures to check those used by the town's traders can still be seen on the wall of the building.

12. The classrooms in Derby Street School were divided by partitions with glass panes in the upper part to allow more daylight into the room. During the darker days, the classrooms were lit with gaslight. These children look as though learning was a very serious business and indeed, there were very few illustrations on the walls to distract their attention. On each desk was an inkwell, as fountain pens were not allowed in schools and ball-point pens had not been invented. Those inkwells reawaken memories of ink-sodden blotting paper and inky fingers and those inevitable blots on exercise books. This would be a fairly small class for the 1920s, because it only had 42 pupils. In many schools the normal number would be between 55 and 60 children. It is not surprising that discipline had to be so strict.

Railway Station, Ormskirk 480

13. The railway first came to Ormskirk in 1849 and by the 1900s, the station had expanded to provide three platforms and a goods siding. It was a very busy station, served by trains from Preston, Southport, Skelmersdale, Liverpool and intermediate stations. Passengers used to wait on the platforms for their connections on other lines and often the Scots express from Liverpool would thunder through, scattering anything left too near the edge of the platform. The engine steaming down the centre line in the picture, was an Aspinall 4-4-0 belonging to the Lancashire and Yorkshire Railway Company, which became part of the London Midland and Scottish Company in 1923.

14. Excursion trains used to run from Ormskirk to Morecambe and Blackpool. The fare to Morecambe was 2s 6d and to Blackpool 1s 9d in the 1930s. In the early morning, a special train left Ormskirk in time to get vegetables and other produce to the various wholesale markets. When the stopping trains drew into the platforms, the newspaper boys and the icecream sellers would shout to attract the attention of the passengers, many of whom used to lean out of the carriage windows to buy gingerbread from Sarah Woods, Ormskirk's popular gingerbread lady. The train standing in the bay on the left of the picture, was a railmotor which served the Ormskirk-Aintree line before it was electrified in 1912. Railmotors were the predecessors of the modern sprinter trains with the engine and the first carriage in one unit.

15. This view of Emmanuel Methodist Church, taken sometime before 1908, shows the Liverpool line at the side of the platform in the station and the old gaslights which lit both the street and the station. Since then, the frontage of Emmanuel has changed little, but now the view of the chimneys of Stanley Street is obscured by the Langham Hall. This hall, which is used for a great variety of activities both by the Methodists and by many other organisations in the town, was opened in 1974.

Emmanuel Church, Ormskirk.

STANLEY STREET ORMSKIRK

16. The shop on the corner of Stanley Street and Wigan Road has long since ceased to be a post office, but a letter box still stands against the garden wall. In the early 1930s, the shop gained a reputation for the scrumptious ice-cream which 'Tosty' Moorcroft used to make during the summer-time. He used to get up as early as three o'clock in the morning to prepare the ice-cream for his customers.

17. Wigan Road has changed very little since 1908 when this postcard was posted, but the houses on the right are now almost derelict, awaiting redevelopment. Behind the bushes, further up the road on the right hand side, were several shops, including Morris's where the townsfolk bought delicious meat and potato pies. Coulton's breadshop and bakery were nearby and the smell of newly baked bread pervaded the whole area. Coulton's had horse-drawn delivery vans which used to deliver bread to the villages and outlying districts. The Scout headquarters further up Wigan Road were opened by Lord Lathom in 1914 and were visited later by Lord and Lady Baden Powell in 1915.

EARL · OF · BEACONSFIELD · MONUMENT
ORMSKIRK

18. Disraeli's monument was erected in 1884 by the Primrose League. On Primrose Day it was the custom for the young Conservatives to put a wreath of primroses onto the statue. It formerly stood in a town in east Lancashire, but its site was needed for another memorial and so it was sold to Ormskirk Conservatives. The building on the left was the Working-men's Institute and Cocoa Rooms. All kinds of functions were held here. For many years, it served as a cinema and the local amateur operatic society made it their home until the 1950s. Election results were often announced from here, after the count had taken place inside the building. On the right can be seen the side of Dr. Lax's surgery, which was once the house of industry — or the workhouse — before it moved to the site of the present hospital.

19. Here is a better view of Dr. Lax's surgery. In the 1820s, when this imposing building was the house of industry, the town's fire engine was housed alongside, on the site of the small cottage. The next tall building is the mansion house, once the town house of the Stanleys of Moor Hall, Aughton. Although they lived so near to Ormskirk, travelling conditions were so bad in the winter months, that they often moved into their town house to avoid the dreary conditions at Moor Hall, which was surrounded by swamps and mossland. They would also use their town house whenever they needed a base in the town for visits to the local theatre, the races, the cockpit or the cold plunge baths at Greetby Hill. The cockpit was conveniently close to the house, between Chapel Street and St. Helens Road.

The Ruff, near Ormskirk

20. These pictures show the Ruff, or Ruff Woods as they are more commonly known. This land was given to the Urban District Council for the use of the people of Ormskirk by Thomas Holcroft, a local magistrate, in 1912. The former quarry was landscaped and made into an attractive woodland which future generations could enjoy.

21. Here we see the Ruff in the process of conversion. Since then, Holcroft's bequest has given endless pleasure to local people, ranging from the children who play hide and seek among the trees and bring their picnics on summer afternoons, to the pensioners who walk their dogs along its shady pathways.

22. In the park in Ruff Lane is a memorial to Sergeant Major Nunnerley of the 17th Lancers who survived the Charge of the Light Brigade. His bravery is the subject of a painting in Manchester Art Gallery, depicting the sergeant major supporting his wounded captain as they struggle away from the battlefield. Nunnerley returned to Ormskirk and built four houses in Greetby Hill, which he called Inkerman, Balaclava, Alma and Sebastopol, to commemorate those battles in the Crimean War. Ormskirk Brass Band used to play in the park on Sunday evenings in the summer and people used to gather to listen to the music. The house with circular bays overlooking this peaceful scene, later became Clarendon School and is now part of the Abbeyfield Sheltered Housing Society.

MARKET DAY ORMSKIRK. R.B.

23. Later, Sergeant Major Nunnerley set up business in 27 Moor Street. This card, posted in 1904, shows his shop next door to the Old Boat Inn, where the landlord was John Birchall. Further down Moor Street were a wine and spirit shop and Rimmer's butcher's whose delicious pork sausages are still remembered. Near the clock tower in the picture can be seen the glass canopy of the Corn Exchange where farmers met to conduct business on market days. On the opposite side of the road was Ablett's shoe shop with a sign high up on the front of the building. In those days, few market traders had the comfort of an awning over their stalls to protect them from the weather. The stalls seem to have had fewer goods and less variety than they do today.

24. This picture of St. Helens Road is interesting because it shows so clearly the difference in the road surfaces. On the left hand side, the roadway has been covered in sand to prevent the horses slipping on the stone sets as they pulled their heavy loads up the slope. On the other side of the road, the sets have not been covered because the slope was downhill and the horses would have had no difficulty. The Council appointed length-men responsible for spreading sand on an appointed stretch of roadway. An old school with external stone steps to the upper storey, used to stand nearby on the right hand side of the road. The buildings behind the trees have now been demolished and modern houses erected on this site.

25. Knowsley Road has changed little. The lady and the little girl in the foreground appear also in the postcard of Stanley Street. Perhaps they were the cameraman's wife and daughter, who had been persuaded to stand at the side of the road to add interest to the picture. Certainly, the lady's hat is more fashionable than many in the other postcards and gives the impression that it was worn especially for the occasion.

26. This horse bus took the people who lived in Bickerstaffe to Ormskirk market. There seems to be another horse bus facing in the opposite direction behind the one with the notice 'Ormskirk Market'. Perhaps the two buses were collecting passengers in Ormskirk for the return journey when this photo was taken.

27. Here we have a busier view of the market, taken sometime before 1905. It is impossible to see what most of the stalls are selling, but one in the forefront has a rack of sheet music propped up behind the stall. Evidently, the cameraman was too late to catch the salesman singing to the crowd and organising a session of community singing before trying to persuade them to buy his sheet music. The building on the left of Ablett's shop in the picture was later demolished and 'The Ship' inn was built in its place. When that inn stopped trading in 1916, the Abletts left their premises, which had also earlier been an inn, 'The Grapes', and moved next door. The sign of the Ship can still be seen above the shop and a hand picking grapes can be seen at the top of the gable on the other property.

For the Best Value in Boots & Shoes you cannot do better than visit

ABLETT'S

ABLETT'S ABLETT

BOOT SHOE 12 ABLETT'S 12 WAREHOUSE

LEADING HOUSE FOR GENUINE BOOTS AND SHOES

Boot and Shoe Manufacturers,
2, MOOR STREET, ORMSKIRK,
And 19, SANDY LANE, SKELMERSDALE.

We are now holding a Splendid Stock of **NEW SEASON'S FOOTWEAR** in all the Latest Shapes and Styles. Our Goods, being of the Highest Class, are justly renowned for their elegant appearance, easy fit, and durability, and are sold at prices considerably below those usually charged for goods of this description.

Ladies' & Gent's Hand-sewn Boots to measure.   Repairs by experienced workmen.

28. This advertisement for Ablett's shoes gives a closer view of the front of their Moor Street shop, before they moved into the premises of the Ship. The ornate classical pilasters at each side of the shop window must have been very attractive. Ablett's had a long tradition as shoemakers in Ormskirk. In the early 1880s, William Ablett already had an established shoe shop and shoe manufacturing business at 17 Aughton Street.

Moor Street, Ormskirk.

29. This photograph, showing the market from the clock tower at the other end of Moor Street, may well have been taken on the same day as the last view of the market. One of the old coaching inns, the King's Arms can be seen further along Moor Street. When the coach arrived from Liverpool, it was driven into the yard at the rear of the King's Arms through a passage-way in Burscough Street. When the passengers had alighted, the coach was driven out, through another passage-way, on to Moor Street, thus avoiding reversing the coach in the inn-yard. The balcony with the two ornamental glass lights was used on special occasions when important visitors appeared for the crowd which gathered below. In the distance can be seen the steep roof of the house which became the Manchester and Liverpool District Bank and which is now the National Westminster Bank.

30. The Prince of Wales visited Ormskirk on 5th July 1921. He was touring Lancashire and Lord Derby was his host while he was in this part of the county. He was not paying an official visit to the town, but as he had to leave his train at Ormskirk, the town authorities took the opportunity to present five local dignitaries to him at a pre-arranged place in front of the Manchester and Liverpool District Bank. Moor Street was lined with ex-servicemen, many of them severely wounded. The Prince left his party and went over to talk to them. As the Ormskirk Advertiser reported: 'All sections of the community flooded into the town... to welcome one who is probably the most popular and best beloved young man in Great Britain today.'

The Cross, Ormskirk

68701. Ⓜ

31. Another view of the King's Arms. It was a tragedy for the town when the planners allowed this magnificent building, dominating the market place, to be demolished, to make way for twentieth century shops with no claim to architectural beauty. Until recently, the canopy with ornate ironwork in front of the Corn Exchange could be seen in Burscough, where it was erected when this site in Ormskirk was redeveloped. The Georgian building on the other side of the road was once the home of the Entwistle family, one of whom, Bertin, became Vice Chancellor of the Duchy of Lancaster in the eighteenth century. After being used for offices, this house became Martins Bank and today houses the Abbey National Building Society. Parrs Bank then occupied the present site of the Halifax Building Society.

32. Yet another view of Moor Street with the market in full swing. By this time, the Ship Inn had been built next to Ablett's shoe shop and the gables of these two buildings dominated the skyline on that side of Moor Street. Behind Ablett's was an old theatre, built towards the end of the 18th century, where dramatic productions were regularly presented. Originally, this theatre was lit by tallow candles on three circular frames suspended from the roof and a man, called 'Tallow Jack' by the noisier elements in the audience, used to snuff the candles when the performance was about to begin. Old theatre bills record that the tickets were sold by Mr. Riddiough the hairdresser, perfumer and whip-maker. The old theatre building could still be seen in 1926, but it had long ceased to be a theatre.

33. In 1876, when it was decided to disband the Court Leet, the clock tower was built on the site of the market cross, using the balance of the funds of the Court Leet and some public subscriptions. The table of tolls at the bottom of the tower, listed the amount each stall-holder had to pay for his stall. For instance, in 1830 out of each sack of barley one measure was paid to the Earl of Derby's toll-gatherer and 1d or 2d was paid for every basket of fruit. Stallholders were charged for their stalls, as they are today, but 'strangers' selling mugs or drapery, paid a higher fee than stallholders from the township. The old fire bell, given to the town by William, Earl of Derby in 1684, can be seen in the turret of the tower.

34. This view up Burscough Street was taken from the clock tower. The white brick features above the shop on the right hand side of the street can still be seen. The passageway to the yard of the Kings Arms ran alongside this building. Halfway up the street was a notice advertising the Maypole for butter and tea. Maypole stores were noted for their moderate prices and were established in many towns. Inside their tiled shops, the grocers used to wear white coats and, after taking the butter out of the wooden butter tubs and weighing it, they would pat it into shape, using a pair of paddles which left a pattern on the slab of butter. On the left hand side of the road was Stoker's first shop and further up was Williams' the grocer's, where the smell of freshly ground coffee filled the air.

35. Here we are looking down Burscough Street to the clock tower. The shop on the left was Wragg's photographer's, and next door was a Georgian house with iron railings which had been the house of a gentry family in the eighteenth century, but which by this time had become the surgery of Dr. Marsden. The large square building was the Wheatsheaf hotel, another of Ormskirk's beautiful buildings. Many of the older residents still treasure memories of descending its elegant staircase after a celebration dinner in one of the upper dining rooms. This hotel also had a stable-yard, which was entered through a passage only about 12ft. wide. Once, a Miss Brocklebank drove a coach and four down Burscough Street and turned them into the Wheatsheaf yard without hesitation, much to the amazement of the male bystanders.

36. The store on the corner is a good example of what happened in the days before permission was needed to erect advertising boards outside stores. The name 'Stoner' appears thirteen times in this photograph, and the second half of the shop is obscured from view! The building on the right with the gable and the coat of arms was the old town hall erected to replace a still older one in 1779. The rooms on the second floor were used for meetings of the Quarter Sessions and the Court Leet and for other public meetings and assemblies. On the ground floor was the mealhouse, where oatmeal, corn and wheat were sold on market days. Also under the sessions room were several butchers' shops, which gave the name of 'The Shambles' to this small area, because of the many slaughter houses at the rear of the shops.

Church Street, Ormskirk.

37. A similar view up Church Street, but by this time, Stoner's had been replaced by Kirk's. Across the road, Clayton's the draper's sold thick black stockings which the girls had to wear for school. Further up, the shop with a corner entrance and a bow-fronted window was Wood's, the chemist's, where in the 1920s Mr. Mc.Kenzie used to peer at this younger customers through pince-nez spectacles. Nearby was the shop of Gladwin, the herbalist, who sold many remedies, sweets, and drinks of dandelion and burdock and nettle 'pop', but perhaps the most popular drink on a bitterly cold winter's day, was his hot sarsaparilla. He provided several tables in the shop and also in the back room, where many of the local youths used to spend their leisure time, playing billiards and drinking Gladwin's herbal drinks.

CHURCH STREET, ORMSKIRK.

38. As we go up Church Street we come to a tea room on the right hand side. Later Dorset's cake shop and tea rooms, a very popular meeting place during the 1930s, stood on this side of Church Street. Another hotel, the Snig's Foot, can be seen near the horse and cart. There have been many attempts to explain this name, but perhaps it was only an old Lancashire joke, for how can a snig – an eel – have a foot? Opposite the Snig's Foot in this card posted in 1911, can be seen the wooden canopy which still shelters the front of the shop of Scott's the butcher's. Behind the ironfounders was the steam corn mill which was destroyed by a huge blaze in 1918. It was reported that nearly 500 boys received canings from their masters for staying too long, watching one of the biggest fires in Ormskirk. The mill was in Besom's yard, so called because besoms were also made there.

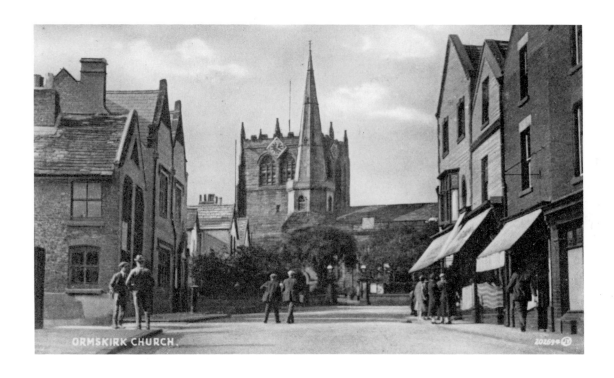

ORMSKIRK CHURCH.

39. As we near the top of Church Street, we can see the old library and Church House. Probably, the library was in the buildings which formerly housed the old Charity School, founded in 1724. Here, the children of the poorer people of Ormskirk were taught to read, primarily so that they could read the Bible, but also to enable them to earn a living more easily so that they would not become a charge on the town's poor rate. The gabled house next to the church is the old vicarage. The cloth blinds stretched across the windows of the shops opposite, were put up whenever the sun shone to prevent the goods in the shop-window fading. They are rarely seen today.

090

ST. PETER'S AND ST. PAUL'S CHURCH, ORMSKIRK

40. Another view of the vicarage taken from the alley-way alongside houses at the top of Church Street. These houses have been converted into shops and their facades of stone blocks have been covered in white paint, but the upper windows remain the same. The vicarage was built in 1528 and various vicars repaired and improved the structure. For instance in 1778, Reverend William Knowles complained to the bishop about the condition of the house. He proposed removing a wattle and daub wall and replacing it with brick to make the wall more durable. Wattle and daub walls remained as interior walls until the building was demolished. The lanterns still remain on the top of the gateposts of the churchyard to light the path up the churchyard.

41. This impressive house was built by the same Reverend Knowles for his wife. He was certain that he would die before her and then she would have to move out of the vicarage to make way for the new vicar. In readiness for that day, he ordered this house to be built. As it happened, she died before he did. The house stood on Burscough Street, north of the intersection of Derby Street. It was another piece of Ormskirk's heritage that the planners allowed to be demolished, this time to make way for the present-day library, another piece of less than memorable architecture.

Old Church, Ormskirk

42. A closer view of the vicarage, showing the pathway which ran down between the vicarage and the church to Coronation Park. This was called the Grove and followed a similar course to today's Park Road. Of course, Park Road is much wider and cuts across the site of the old vicarage. On this path and slightly behind the vicarage, was a row of old cottages, also victims of the construction of Park Road. Today, the small park in front of the churchyard stands on part of the site of these old cottages.

Ormskirk Church.

43. Down that pathway can be seen the backs of those cottages, their tiny windows being a sign of their considerable age. On the other side of the path another cottage is visible, but that too was demolished and on its site the modern vicarage was built. The old bricks of the cottage can still be seen in the vicarage garden wall.

Ormskirk Church, Tower and Steeple.

44. This card posted in 1905, is another view of The Grove showing more clearly the cottage on the other side of the path. The hedges and the two garden gates stress the rural nature of the town at the turn of the century. There was no need for immense car parks and wide tarmac roads in those days.

PARISH CHURCH, ORMSKIRK

45. Here the back of the vicarage can be seen overlooking parkland where the children are playing on swings. The chimney visible at the extreme left hand side of the picture, belongs to the row of cottages which still stands, untouched by modern development, overlooking the extended graveyard.

46. Those cottages in the Grove overlooked Coronation Park, shown in this delightful view in which everyone seems to be wearing their Sunday-best clothes. Although this picture looks so casual at first glance, the photographer has obviously posed the little group around the park bench. The little girl in all her finery and the boy in a cap would never have perched so precariously on the arm of the bench, unless they had been asked to do so. The pile of discarded clothing in the foreground presumably belongs to the lad with a straw hat, preparing to paddle in the pond. It looks as if he too had been moved to create a more attractive picture.

The Park, Ormskirk.

47. Another view on a quieter, autumn day. In the 1930s, Coronation Park was the site of many children's picnics organised after the Whitsuntide processions through the town. The town brass band also used to play here during the summer time. Nowadays, the park is used in the summer as a venue for Ormskirk Gala and the great brick hulk of the Park Pool dominates this view. The shelter has gone and even the trees behind it have been removed. A large concrete pipe intended as a children's play ground, has been erected in their place.

48. Wragg, the Ormskirk photographer, took this photograph of a football team with their trainers. The high, starched collars on two of the youths and the watch chains sported by the older men, set the date to the early twentieth century, but it has been impossible to identify anyone in the photograph. The writing on the ball 'Central 1906-7' should jog the memory of some senior citizens of Ormskirk.

49. Dyers Lane has changed little since this card was posted in 1910. New houses stand where the washing is hanging out and the sets on the roadway are now covered in tarmac, making a much quieter surface. The noise made by horses and carts as they trundled over sets, used to disturb people who were ill and so, whenever anyone was seriously ill, straw used to be spread over the sets to deaden the sound. This was also done outside hospitals, especially in busy towns.

TOWN END ORMSKIRK

50. Town End, at the beginning of Prescot Road, has changed. The leafy garden is now the site of more houses and the row of cottages with no gardens, together with the tall Georgian house, have been demolished to make way for St. Anne's Social Centre. It is possible that the tall building was the house built by Father Bulmer in 1746, after the library in his home in the centre of Ormskirk had been burnt by rioters. The old Catholic church of St. Oswald's, which served for many years as a school for Catholic children before the Hants Lane School was opened, stood behind the high brick wall. This card was posted in 1912.

51. A slightly earlier view of Town End, taken about 1908 from the opposite direction. Again the cottages, the Georgian house and the high brick wall can be seen. Later a brewery was built on the right hand side of the road, but now most of that property and land is used by the Council as a depot.

ST. ANNE'S CHURCH, ORMSKIRK.

52. New houses have also been built on the corner opposite St. Anne's Catholic Church. The signpost no longer stands on that corner and Ormskirk gasometer has now disappeared, after long service in the town. The gas company was founded in 1835 and supplied the streets of Ormskirk with lighting from the 1880s.

ST. ANNES R.C. CHURCH, ORMSKIRK.

53. This interior view of St. Anne's Church dates from the days of the First World War. In recent times, another altar table has been erected in front of the high altar, to enable the priest to serve Mass facing the congregation. A wooden reading desk also stands now at the front of the church.

54. These buildings of the grammar school remain unchanged since the alterations in 1907, but now they are surrounded by extensions of various kinds, including a large sports hall. The land on the opposite side of Mill Street was used as playing fields at the time of this picture, but now it is covered with classrooms and a small playground.

55. This group of scholars and staff of the grammar school dates from 1930. Among the masters in the complete group, of which this is only a part, were the Reverend Bate, Mr. Boswell, Mr. Chippendale, Mr. Cliffe, Mr. Green and Mr. Hamilton and among the mistresses were Miss Thornton and Miss Robinson.

56. This house, Claremont, has been used as classrooms for the grammar school since 1960. Originally the house belonged to Henry Jones, a rope master, whose initials can be seen on a plaque above the right-hand bay window. His rope works were alongside the grammar school grounds and a small winding house still exists beside the house. The Rope Walk stretched between Wigan Road and Ruff Lane and is remembered in the name of the Roper's Arms. Rope making had been an important industry in the town from Tudor times until comparatively recently. Ropes used to be in great demand for sailing boats, horse-drawn carts and other innumerable uses, both on the farm and in the home. Originally, the industry used hemp, which was grown extensively in the damp fields of West Lancashire, to make the ropes.

COTTAGE LANE NR. ORMSKIRK

57. These houses on Cottage Lane have lost their rural outlook. Most of the trees have gone; the railings and gateposts have been altered and they are now surrounded by houses of various ages, built to fill every available piece of land. The modern development of Redgate extends behind this row and Redgate meets Cottage Lane at the corner in the background of this picture. Now, beyond the trees on the right, in the background of the picture, is an electrician's shop. The path going through the hedge on the right of the picture, skirts the side of the shop and joins County Road, which did not exist at the time this photograph was taken.

BROOKACRE NR. ORMSKIRK

58. This view of the same cottages was taken from that path, near to its present junction with County Road. Originally the path wound between hedges and across fields to the church. Today, its course can still be followed from Cottage Lane to County Road, across Coronation Park to Park Road. In the early decades of this century, the fields to the right of the picture used to be flooded during the winter months and if there was a continuous hard frost, the youths of the town used to skate and play ice hockey on the ice. This picture of Brookacre was posted in 1912.

59. This lady presents many problems. She cannot be identified, nor can the place where she kept her hens. All that is known is that the photograph was taken in the Ormskirk area. I wonder if any readers will be able to trace the origin of this delightful picture.

Ormskirk. Aughton Street.

60. Now we return to the market place, but this time we are approaching it from Aughton Street. Again the King's Arms dominates the scene. The frontage and entrance door of the Post Office remain much the same today as they were in those days, but the original iron railings and the gate posts have gone and have been replaced by their modern equivalents. Probably, the iron railings were taken in the 1940s to help the war effort along with many others from around the town. In the centre of the picture, a young woman can be seen spreading lengths of cloth on the roadway. It is a mystery why she was doing that; perhaps she was going to put her wares on the cloth to display them.

Aughton Street, Ormskirk

61. The Talbot was another old coaching inn. One traveller visiting the town in 1790, reported: 'Scarcely had we alighted at the Talbot Inn, when we were offered by half a dozen fair hands together, little packets of gingerbread.' This would have taken place in the yard behind the inn, where there were stables for the horses. These stables have now been converted into small workshops behind Park Hall. The fish stones where a man is sitting in the picture, were the subject of an order made by the Court Leet in the seventeenth century. No-one was to sell fish anywhere else in the market but from the fish stones, so that the smell and nuisance could be isolated in that part of the square.

MARKET DAY, ORMSKIRK.

62. This view up Aughton Street was taken from the corner of Park Road. On the left hand side are two lodging houses where workers staying temporarily in the town, lived. The Post Office has a small 'public telephone' notice outside, but the large advertisement of Williams', the tailor's, dominates the whole scene. A later generation of the same family still has a men's outfitter's shop in the town today. The huge pair of spectacles outside a shop nearer to the clock tower, leaves no doubt as to where the optician's shop is.

Ormskirk Market

The Wrench Series No. 1502

63. The first shop on the right is a china shop known as 'Muggy Lees', where it could almost be guaranteed that any broken cup or saucer could be matched and replaced. Next door is the White Bull, yet another of Ormskirk's hostelries, and beyond that is the shop of James Iddon, fishmonger, immediately across the pavement from the fishstones. Another inn, the Fleece, where the Umpire coach used to stop to pick up passengers, stands next to the shop of John Bell, the boot manufacturer. Later, the Fleece was pulled down and Barclays Bank moved into the new premises.

64. Closer to the clock, we can see Mawdsley's shop with Ormskirk gingerbread advertised across the facade. The smell of roasting coffee and smoked bacon which met the customers on entering the shop, is still remembered by many of Ormskirk's senior citizens. In the forefront of the market is a plant stall similar to those in the market today. In the early years of the century, the market used to stay open until eleven o'clock. The stalls were lit with paraffin flares, a highly dangerous method of lighting. It was the accepted pastime of many townsfolk after their evening meal to gather round the pot stall, where the 'mugman' used to entertain them with his patter, as he tried to persuade them to buy.

65. Yet another picture of the clock tower, but this one taken in 1905, gives us a better view of Mawdsley's shop. A telegraph post can be seen high above the roof. In 1903 there were only 49 phones in Ormskirk and most of those were in business premises, only three being in private houses. At that time, the only public call office was in 50 Burscough Street. A drinking fountain at the base of the clock tower originally supplied water for thirsty passersby. Possibly, the water came from the stream which at one time ran down the centre of Moor Street and Aughton Street to the brook at Town End. In the mid-nineteenth century the stream became very contaminated and so it was culverted.

66. Further down Aughton Street was the boys' school. This group of their teachers was taken in the late 1920s. George Harrison, now in his nineties, is second from the right on the back row.

67. Here Mr. Harrison is teaching morris dancing to a group of boys from Aughton Street School. The boy at the back is providing the music with his mouth organ. All the boys — and their teacher — are concentrating on their performance. No smiles can be spared for the cameraman. Mr. Harrison, who still teaches country dancing in the town, is known throughout England for his work in popularising English folk dancing. The composer and band leader, Jimmy Shand, often played for dances at which Mr. Harrison was the caller and has written several tunes for him, including 'George Harrison's Reel'.

68. One of the younger classes at Aughton Street School. They must have recently moved from Derby Street School, where the boys stayed until they were seven years old. The elderly teacher with his starched wing collar and bowler hat, looks weighed down with the responsibility and cares of educating his young charges.

MARKET DAY, AUGHTON ST., ORMSKIRK.

69. The view up Aughton Street from the school in the late 1920s. In the foreground is Evans' drapery shop. The Fleece has been demolished and Barclays Bank with its twin dormers, has been erected on the site. The old stables behind the Talbot Hotel, were no longer needed and the sign 'Garage' over the passage-way to the inn-yard indicates that the stables have been converted for a more modern use. The notice for the cattle auction behind the Talbot, also proclaims that other changes have occurred. The twice-yearly cattle and horse fair which originally took place in Moor Street, has been abandoned and an auction has taken its place. The banner hanging out from one of the shops, also heralds a change in photography. Kodak films are now available for the man in the street.

70. This boy and his father are flying a kite on Ravenscroft, where there were tennis courts and an athletic ground with a stand for spectators in the 1920s. This ground extended behind Brook Lane and Bridge Street to the railway line. Today it is remembered in the name of Ravenscroft Avenue. The houses in the background are in Chapel Street, and the property on the right behind the tree, is Chapel Street dairy, now the premises of Hannah's Pies.

71. Southport Road has changed little since 1908 when this postcard was written. The stone wall on the right has been lowered; many of the trees have been felled and the large house in the centre background has been demolished. On its site, the new cul-de-sac Rosecroft Close has been built and its former gardens are now part of the grounds of the Comrades Club. Ormskirk's war memorial stands at the side of the road in front of the Club today. This road was known as Bark House Hill in the eighteenth century.

72. Looking up Southport Road, again little has changed. The ivy no longer covers the house on the right and the iron railings have gone. The roof of the Drill Hall, which now serves as the Civic Hall, can be seen over the roofs of the houses on the left.

GROWN WITH HADFIELD'S SPECIAL POTATO MANURE.

Grown by Mr. E. Threlfall, Bangors Green, Ormskirk. A sound, healthy crop, weighed 18½ tons per acre

73. This view of harvesting the potato crop near Ormskirk is a reminder of how much the farmers used to depend on horses and a large labour force. Men came from Ireland to help with the harvest and today their temporary homes − often now in a ruinous condition − can be seen on many of the farms in the Ormskirk district. These buildings were known locally as 'Paddy shacks' or 'Paddy shants'. At the height of the potato harvest, children were also recruited to help with the work and schools often closed for a week. The baskets used for the potatoes, were made from the willows which grew on the damp mossland. The bonnets worn by the women, were very popular among country-women at the turn of the century and they too, were made locally by seamstresses.

Market Place.

74. The importance of horses in the town for all kinds of transport is also well illustrated in this view of the market. They were needed to pull carts of all descriptions, ranging from brewers' drays to traps. The children, wearing pinafores in the picture, are on their way home from school, while the lady in a large, white apron is probably a stallholder in the market. On the right hand side of the road, next to Gilbey's wine store, are the offices of Stretch and Idle, auctioneers and valuers. Bill-boards stand on the pavement outside their premises, advertising future sales. The horse and cart in front of those offices are standing on the weighing machine, used to weigh loads of coal and suchlike things.

75. In this final bird's eye view of the market, a horse pulling a carriage, is being driven by a coachman with a top-hat and the passengers are shading themselves from the sun with parasols. A coach is parked outside the King's Arms. The gentry have come to town.

76. No comment!